RUSSIAN POET WITH AN UZBEK HEART

TRANSLATION OF POEMS BY ALEKSANDR FEINBERG

MAFTUNA ABDURASULOVA

Made with ♥ on the Notion Press Platform
www.notionpress.com

This book will be about Aleksandr Feinberg`s
life shortly together with his some poems,
translated bye the auther Abdurasulova
Maftuna. Aleksandr Feinberg is not only writer,
but also he is translator of some Uzbek poems.

Contents

Foreword   *vii*

Acknowledgements   *ix*

1. Russian Poet With An Uzbek Heart   1

Foreword

It is no exaggeration to say that Uzbek literature is made up of
such a wide variety of gems that each of them has a delicate ring,
each of them serves as a school of great skill for us. It can be
said that the works of our people and our youth, who occupy a
deep place in the hearts of our nation and our youth with their
masterpieces and priceless works, the works of our writers who
shake the world with their pen, and the works of our translators,
who are happy to help us enjoy world literature, can be said to be
an incomparable heritage for us. One of such great talents is writer,
poet and translator Alexander Arkadyevich Feinberg. Let's say it in
one word: "The heart is an Uzbek Russian poet". When we observe
the path of the poet's life, we can see that he faced many difficulties,
and even in such situations, he picked up the pen again with his
literary will. This proves that his body and soul are equally strong.
You can see the magical paths of creativity traveled by the heart of
a person who painted the life of a great poet. I got a lot of useful
information while studying these paths of creativity. As I read the
charming lines of his poems, I came across feelings that made my
heart flutter. His work is effective, and his poems are soulful. In this
process, the reader will have a special feeling. Especially his poem
"Love" left a great impression on me. During the translation of his
creative legacy, I realized how great a school of skills his footprints
will be for us. We are also in the process of carrying out extensive
work to spread his work widely to Uzbek readers.

Acknowledgements

Contents:

Introduction..3
Short Biography of Aleksandr Feinberg...............................4
List of his literary works..6
Translation of writers some poems 7
Moon Landscape 7
Width..8
Love..8
Painter..9

CHAPTER ONE

Russian Poet with an Uzbek heart

Biography

Alexander Feinberg Arkadevich - Russian poet, People's Poet of Uzbekistan. Alexander Feinberg is undoubtedly one of the brightest stars in the sky of poets of Uzbekistan. His work is very colorful. He is the author of collections published in Tashkent, Moscow and St. Petersburg. Scripts of feature films belong to him. By the decree of the President of Russia, the poet of Uzbekistan Alexander Arkadevich Feinberg was awarded the 2008 Pushkin Medal.

Alexander Arkadevich Feinberg was born on November 2, 1939 in Tashkent - after his parents moved to Novosibirsk in 1937.

He spent his childhood on the former Zhukovsky Street. After completing the seven-year school, Alexander Feinberg entered the Tashkent topographic technical school. After finishing the technical school, he goes to Tajikistan for military service. Then, he graduated from Tashkent University (now Tashkent State National University) from the Journalism Department of the Faculty of Philology, and worked for a large number of students. 1961 married I. N.

Koval.

He is the author of fifteen poetry books. Also, based on his scripts, four full-length feature films and more than twenty multiplex films were shot. He translated epics and poems of Alisher Navoi, as well as poems of other modern Uzbek poets into Russian. His poems are published in the magazines "Smena", "Yunost" ("Youth"), "Novyy mir" ("New World"), "Zvezda Vostoka" ("Eastern Star"), "Novaya Volga" ("New Wave"). and published in periodicals of foreign countries such as USA, Canada and Israel.

In 1999, on the occasion of the 12th anniversary of the death of the "Pakhtakor" football team in a tragic plane crash, a film called "Their ball field is in the sky" was shot based on his script. The lyrics of the song in the film were written in 1979 by Alexander Feinberg.

For several years, A. A. Feinberg led the workshop of young writers of Uzbekistan in Tashkent. He was also considered a member of the Union of Writers of Uzbekistan.

2004 poet A.A. Feinberg was awarded the Pushkin Medal by decree of the President of Russia. He received this high award for his outstanding contribution to the development of cultural relations with the Russian Federation and the preservation of the Russian language and Russian culture. Aleksandr Fainberg is undoubtedly one of the brightest stars in the poetry dome of Uzbekistan. His creativity is amazing. He is the author of thirteen poetry collections published in Tashkent, Moscow and St. Petersburg.

He wrote seven feature film scripts, the most notable of which are: "Under the bluest sky", "House under the hot sun", "Caught in Kandahar", he is also the author of 18 multiplex films. is also His prose is very interesting.

An excellent translator, Feinberg revealed many works of famous Uzbek poets to the Russian-speaking reader. In Moscow, Erkin Vahidov's epic "Rebellion of Souls" was published, and in Tashkent, a collection of poems by Abdulla Oripov and Khosiyat Rustamova, Sirojiddin Said and Amon Matchon, "A Gala of White Birds" was published.

Feinberg's poems have a sparkling sense of humor. In the epic "Rubai Tori" he described the unchanging cuisine of the Uzbek tea house through laughter in such a way that it cannot be read without a smile on his face.

Alexander Arkadevich Feinberg died on October 14, 2009 in Tashkent.

List of his literary works:
* "Bicycle Tracks" (1965),
* "Etude" (1967),
* "Sonia" (1969),
* "Poems" (1977),
* "Far Bridges" (1978),
* "Seal of Heaven" (1982)
* "Short Wave" (1983),
* "Yomator" (1984),
* "Free Sonnets" (1990)
* "Sheet" (2008)
* The 2-volume collection of works collected by the author was published after the death of the creator.

Translation of writers some poets..

MOON LANDSCAPE
Standing on the sky's edge,
The fisherman thinks alone and silent.
Bowing the net on the ledge,
The creature shines in the moonlight.

Hanging stars in the night,
Silver boat,handful-handful of dice.
Burying the boats in the light,
Polished rivers,palm-palm of dice .

WIDTH
What beautiful fields and grass,
My mother's footsteps-pain limitless.
Now,my life is on its kness,
Forever in front of my mam's goodless.

LOVE
I am swimming, love , far away,
Smoke rises from the fire,
I am leaving in this beach today,
I will throw the anchor on the shore.

The star can kiss you ,
Realated to water blue.
Running waves is a large ,

River's bottom is a literary gorge.

The flow along the river goes,
Looking at the sky – the birds,
Feeling of separation – waves,
Holding each other as they feel.

Your slippery face is hot ,
Invisible fire smoke,
Behind the clouds is the shore,
"I am sorry" it doesn't fit in the sky.

PAINTER
Leonardo, always in the smoke
Sometimes dumb like a fish,
Sometimes stupidly drunk,
He paints again on bare sackcloth

You look everywhere,, it's imaginary
A visible iron piece from the window frame
Better a poor horse than no horse is worthy

There is niether joy in the house, nor budget
If the wheel rotation means old age
A broken plate that flies into a bucket
And you are crying by the window stage

Ooh Leonardo, here's your luck
Hurry to draw a picture of her

She is crying beautifully by the curtain tag.